ABDUCTION

THE MINIVAN MURDERS

by RJ Parker

ABDUCTION
THE MINIVAN MURDERS

by RJ Parker

ISBN-13: *978-1987902396*
ISBN-10: *1987902394*

Copyrights

"This is a work of nonfiction. No names have been changed, no characters invented, no events fabricated."

– RJ Parker

More True Crime Books in the Kindle Store:

rjpp.ca/RJ-PARKER-BOOKS

Table of Contents

Introduction

In the world of crime, while each case is heinous and a blow to humanity, there are some cases which leave a mark on not just the victims but everybody who comes across them. The United States alone have been responsible for a few of the most notorious and horrific killers of all time. Ted Bundy, Jeffrey Dahmer and many other serial killers have been caught and convicted for committing gruesome murders and subjecting their innocent victims to torture. A number of the killers who have made headlines across the world have been male, as noted by many psychologists analyzing their behavior. When it comes to female serial killers, there have been several but nowhere near as many as their counterparts. These females have many times worked with a partner, usually male, joining forces to carry out violent acts and torture.

The deadly serial killer couples that shook the world by their grisly and heinous crimes include Michael and Suzan Carson, Doug Clark and Carol M. Bundy, Paul Bernardo and Karla Homolka, and Fred and Rosemary West, just to name a few.

As evident from the above-mentioned twosomes, female serial killers have worked with their male equivalent and gone on to kill several innocent men, women and children. During the

1940s, Raymond Fernandez and Martha Beck, termed as the 'Lonely Hearts Killers', took the lives of three women and a child. The killers' involvement was also suspected in more than twenty murder cases across Michigan and New York.

It surprised psychological analysts and human behavior researchers everywhere that women were partaking in evil acts of violence and pain. After numerous studies between the relationships of serial killer couples, it was implied that the relationship between two partners was somewhat similar to a submissive and a dominant one. Either the male or female was responsible for the execution and torture of the victim, whilst the other scouted possible targets. Despite years of research and studies, analysts were mostly lost for an explanation as to what prompted the serial killer couples to torture and murder innocent people.

While serial killers have been in existence since before the time of "Jack the Ripper", there has been a decline in their numbers over the years. Throughout the early to mid-twentieth-century, America experienced one of its worst criminal periods as far as serial crimes are concerned. The wave continued on to the late 1990s and even into the Twenty-first century. One of the most notorious killing pairs that surfaced during this time was Michelle Michaud and James Daveggio.

Biography

James Anthony Daveggio, also known as 'Froggie,' and Michelle Lyn Michaud were 42 and 43 years of age, respectively, at the time of their conviction in 2002. When news of their crimes made global headlines, researchers and psychologists began to dig deeper into their history and background. It was determined that Daveggio was born on July 27, 1960, in San Francisco, California, while Michaud, also referred to as 'Mickie' by her partner, was a year older than him.

Since an early age, both Daveggio and Michaud encountered difficulties with their family lives, especially during their adolescent years. In 1974, when he was 14 years old, Daveggio was questioned during the investigation of Cassie Riley's murder. The 13-year-old girl was found near an embankment by a creek in Union City, California. Upon investigation, it was revealed that the girl had died due to drowning, and there was evidence of severe assault, with injuries to the head and neck. While rape could not be determined, the investigators found her clothes disheveled. As the case progressed, investigating officials found evidence of James Daveggio being present on the scene when Cassie Riley disappeared. Later on, he even claimed that she had been his girlfriend.

The investigators did not pay close attention to his claims as a few other boys had also gone on record to state something similar. A number of analysts deem this incident the beginning of Daveggio's long violent history. At the scene of Riley's murder, the police found sneaker prints of a size 10 shoe, which helped them come up with possible suspects. Eyewitnesses also stated that, before her disappearance, Riley had been seen talking to a young boy with a green shirt with a sleeve patch. However, this did not lead to any conclusive results.

In May 1975, almost six months after the atrocious killing, the police convicted Marvin Mutch of Cassie's murder. Much later it was revealed that Mutch had been falsely convicted as his prints did not match the evidence found at the scene of the crime nor were any links to Riley determined. Mutch spent 41 years in prison and was only recently released.

Many believe that the reason Daveggio managed to get away unscathed was his sister's false alibi, wherein she stated that her brother had been present at home during the time of the murder. Since that time, his violent behavior began to slowly progress. He would get into fights in his high school and gravely injure his fellow students. He stole a car belonging to a girlfriend's mother and often got physically violent with young girls. Soon enough, Daveggio was sent to live with his birth father in Pasadena, California.

Even that did not make much of a difference, and he was back with his mother after a short stay. He was sent to a juvenile detention center in Alameda County for robbing a gas station. During the detention period, he acquired his nickname, 'Froggie', and also met a friend, Michael Ihde, who shared the same twisted perversions as he did. Most likely, Ihde was the person responsible for triggering his violent sexual fantasies that soon eclipsed his entire thought process. Michael Ihde also went on to become a killer and a serial rapist.

Once out of the juvenile center, Daveggio worsened in his ways. He was known to be involved in several robberies, abductions and rape cases. While initially, the rape charges were dropped due to the victim's statement which could not prove him guilty, Daveggio eventually was arrested and put through a psychiatric evaluation. He was officially considered as a sex offender and flagged by the Sex Offender Registry. However, whenever he moved, he kept his whereabouts hidden from the authorities.

Soon enough, James Daveggio was caught again for picking up a female police officer posing as a prostitute and offering her money. He was sent to the California Medical Facility, situated within Vacaville, and fined heavily for drinking and disorderly conduct. Despite that, Daveggio managed to secure his release shortly and moved to Sacramento. He dropped out of high school and then married his pregnant girlfriend, Becky. The relationship did not last long due to Daveggio's habitual gambling and heavy drinking. In Sacramento, he joined a motorcycle gang called The Devil's Horsemen. It is commonly understood that during his time in Sacramento, James Daveggio, met Michelle Michaud. These future serial killers bonded over their mutual appreciation of violent sexual acts.

Michaud, at the time, was already a prostitute and frequently experimented with various drugs. After a string of failed relationships, Michelle Michaud was his first steady partner. As experts determined, Michaud also came from a similar background as Daveggio and might have been assaulted by her father. At the age of 16, she had run away from home and moved in with a physically abusive drug dealer. Michaud entered prostitution and took multiple partners before meeting Daveggio. She was apparently impressed with his position as a gang member, believing herself to be protected in his presence. Prior to their meeting in 1996 or 1997, Michaud had worked in a massage parlor and had been arrested several times.

Michaud and Daveggio established a relationship with the latter moving into her house after a short period of dating. She tried her best to impress him but, after a while, nothing was good enough. However, Michaud stayed with Daveggio and even tried to build a family with him.

The bar where he worked was robbed just before Christmas and, while his involvement in the crime was not proven until later, he was fired for getting violent with the customers. After that, he took a job in security, working as a guard during the day. His interest in Michaud began to decline, and he would often bring other girlfriends to the house.

Daveggio's partner allowed the presence of various women in his life, believing that it would keep him happy and content. Despite that, his behavior began to worsen, and he became increasingly violent and abusive towards Michaud. He would often lock her up and leave her for days, all the while subjecting her to physical violence and savage sex. Both Michaud and Daveggio were into drugs, and their expensive habit soon created a mountain of debt for them. In order to lessen the financial burden, they let their friend deal drugs from the premises. Soon enough, their luck ran out. The authorities discovered that their home was a place of illegal drug activity. During the law enforcement investigation, Daveggio's status as a sex offender was discovered and, as there were children in the house, he was ordered to move out.

At this same time, Daveggio was also kicked out of The Devil's Horsemen due to his involvement in a burglary. Accordingly, this was when he began to exhibit curiosity in serial killers, reading books about them and being particularly fascinated with Gerald Gallego. Drawing inspiration from Gallego, Daveggio managed to persuade Michaud to kidnap her daughter's friend and lure her to an isolated place. He assaulted and raped her, while his partner was also involved in the act. This was the beginning of the crime spree the deadly killers were about to commence.

Soon after this incident, 20-year-old Alicia Paredes had been walking home one night when a green minivan stopped. Froggie hopped out while Mickie was at the wheel. He grabbed Alicia and tossed her in the van. Daveggio raped her while Mickie looked on. They then tossed her out like a sack of trash. Alicia went directly to the police. Paredes had heard him refer to Michaud as 'Mickie,' and she worked with a sketch artist to identify the criminals. While it was determined that the driver was female and the abductor male, the investigating officials still came up short of arresting the perpetrators.

The green minivan belonged to Michaud and soon became a torture chamber for her partner. He installed hooks and ropes in the vehicle, removing the seats to accommodate his gruesome criminal plans. Both Michaud and Daveggio began to play out their perverse fantasies, kidnapping more women and forcing them to participate in sexual acts. The duo's further victims included Michaud's daughter and five other girls across the state of Nevada. Psychologists and analysts across the globe failed to identify the root cause of this increasingly violent behavior which terrorized the victims.

Daveggio did not even spare his own 16-year-old daughter, who told a grand jury that on Thanksgiving Day 1997, her father asked if she would like to help kidnap a victim off the street and kill her. He called it "hunting", she said.

During their spree, Michaud was apprehended by police on charges of falsifying checks and booked into the Douglas County Jail in November 1997. She was released shortly; however, after which the two went on to resume their activities. While her stint in jail had brought her onto the radar of the authorities, both she and Daveggio escaped arrest until the rape and murder of Vanessa Samson on December 2, 1997.

The police began to investigate the two more

thoroughly, taking statements from Michaud's daughter and her friend, both of whom were rape and assault victims. While the officers managed to get a location on the couple, they failed to make an arrest. One by one, victims were discovered, yet at the time, Vanessa Samson had not been killed.

As an arrest warrant was issued for both Michaud and Daveggio, the couple made their way into Pleasanton, California. Daveggio's desire to kill kept becoming stronger until he finally asked Michaud to bring him a victim. Unfortunately, 22-year-old Vanessa Samson caught the eye of the deadly twosome and was subjected to physical assault, rape and torture. Her body was dumped over an embankment. Soon afterward, the authorities tracked down the killers to a motel and managed to arrest them on charges of assault and kidnapping for starters.

At this time, Vanessa Samson's body had not been discovered. It wasn't until ropes and other evidence of the crime surfaced that the investigation took a turn.

The serial killers were linked to a possible murder and then Samson's body was discovered. They were both charged with rape, torture and murder. After a trial, Michaud and Daveggio were sentenced to death while analysts grappled with the acts of 'pure evil' that they had perpetrated. The relationship between the two became a subject of many studies with psychologists trying to figure out which was the dominant and which was the submissive. Numerous accounts were taken and pieced together, eventually leading to the conclusion that both were equally involved in the assault and torture of innocent victims, including their own family members.

Later on, when they were finally apprehended by the police and details of their case began to make rounds, more information regarding the background of the killers surfaced. Daveggio had always tried to emulate his father, and according to one of his wives, idolized him in every sense. His father had multiple failed relationships and married quite a few times. While this way of life worked out for him, Daveggio could not keep himself from spiraling out of control. He displayed sociopathic tendencies from an early age and was unable to keep away from trouble. It was evident to the people around him that James Daveggio did not care about anyone and lacked self-control when it came to interacting with the opposite gender.

Perhaps the lack of a father figure in his life was a huge factor in his behavioral problems. It was also the reason why, despite his frequent run-ins with the law, he was always protected by his mother, Darlene. As a teenager, Daveggio would get into trouble in his neighborhood for displaying violent behavior or getting caught up in a burglary, yet Darlene always came up with an excuse to prove him innocent. For her, James Daveggio was a harmless child who had minor problems while growing up.

Further on, when the rumors began to circulate that he may be involved in several abductions and physical assaults, Darlene still managed to convince herself that her son could not be at fault.

One of Daveggio's classmates remembered him as a boy who did not stand out amongst the crowd at first glance. She recalled that he was a 'shy and quiet boy' who had bright blue eyes and blond hair.

While in high school, Daveggio managed to keep his twisted sexual fantasies hidden and even attracted a few girls. However, this was a short-term phase that quickly ended when he made the move to Pleasanton. He constantly rebelled in his new school and failed to make any new friends due to his increasing aggressiveness. It was in a juvenile detention center that he met Michael Ihde who truly connected with Daveggio like no one ever had before. Ihde shared the same dark fantasies and penchant for violence as him, prompting a strong bond between the two.

Both Ihde and Daveggio began to spend their time together and, soon enough, their influence rubbed off on each other. With the progress of time, Daveggio moved away and joined the biker gang, while Ihde went on to become a serial rapist and murderer.

After going on a spree in Bay Area, California, Michael Ihde was finally caught and charged with several murders of young women. It was during his conviction that Daveggio's name surfaced and their connection became known to the authorities. However, at the time, Daveggio was still active as a gang member and only involved in petty crimes. The police kept him on their radar as a sex offender but did not pursue him due to lack of evidence.

Daveggio's life changed when he met Michelle Michaud, but it is unclear as to who was the driving force behind their murder and rape spree. A few psychological experts have shed light on the possibility of Daveggio suffering from a personality disorder. They say that there were two personalities that Daveggio was caught in between: the shy and quiet one, and the other loud mouthed and aggressive side. It could have been Michelle's entry into his life which prompted his aggressive personality to become prominent and eclipse his rational thought. However, at the end, the argument can be made that Daveggio was a sociopath from the very beginning. Michaud might have helped him execute his twisted plans later on, but it was only a matter of time before his violent side got the better of him.

The backseat of the minivan was removed and ropes were attached inside to restrain their victims

Michelle Michaud

There are varying accounts of how Michelle Michaud and James Daveggio actually met. One popular version of their meeting describes Michaud running into Daveggio at a bar in 1996 and becoming instantly attracted to his biker gang status as well as muscular looks. It has been stated that when Daveggio joined the gang, he got heavily tattooed, dyed his hair and stole a Harley Davidson to become initiated. Michaud was working as a high level prostitute when she walked into a bar, Bobby Joe's, with a friend and took one look at Daveggio, who was a bartender there, and announced that she 'wanted him'.

While this account could very well be true, Michaud later contradicted this version and narrated the story of their first meeting herself. According to her, she met Daveggio on Halloween in 1996. They were introduced through mutual friends and met to discuss some problems her daughters were having with some friend of his. Daveggio stepped in and assured Michaud that he would speak to the man involved and 'take care' of the problem. It was implied that due to his increasingly aggressive streak, he might have done much more than just talked to the man involved.

Soon afterwards, Daveggio became interested in the fiery red head, who at first rebuffed his advances. She told him that her work had introduced her to the worst in men and she no longer wanted to be with one. Michaud also spoke openly about staying in her line of work and not wanting to change whatsoever. Despite that, Daveggio pursued her and insisted that they see each other. After a short while, she relented and they began to date.

Michaud did not expect it to become anything serious; however, against all odds, she found herself falling for him. He treated her like a lady and did not bring her background as a prostitute up again. While most of his teeth had been knocked out, Michaud found him attractive and was drawn to his blue eyes. Daveggio somehow managed to charm her with his mannerism and muscular build which provided Michelle with a sense of security. Despite her aggressive demeanor, Michaud craved protection and security that she lacked since an early age. It was implied that her father could be the reason behind her going into prostitution and she had never had a childhood while growing up.

Perhaps the couple's tumultuous family background had been a major factor into bringing them together. In the early days of their relationship, Daveggio earned Michaud's respect and acceptance. He stood on her behalf against family members and friends who constantly shunned her for her lifestyle. At the same time, Daveggio also managed to drive away the people who warned Michaud of his aggressive and violent nature.

There were a few people in Michelle Michaud's circle of friends who told her that James Daveggio was not good for her. Just like his third wife, Donetta, she also did not listen to the warnings of her friends and family. She had become so enamored by him that minor indiscretions on his part did not matter to her anymore. According to one of her statements, he was the kind of man who demanded 'respect from your family for you.' She also said that Daveggio stood up to her family and did not let anyone chase him out of her life which showed his commitment to her and their life together. Michaud stated that 'he had been nothing but good to her.'

At first look, the two could not have been more different in their demeanor. Right from his school days, Daveggio had managed to subdue his true nature by appearing shy and quiet to girls during initial meetings. He had very deep blue eyes that also made him come across as someone who was engaging and slightly attractive. Michaud, on the other hand, was a strong-headed, loud-mouthed and self-confident woman. There was nothing even remotely shy about her, and she could most probably walk into any room with ease.

The people who initially came across the couple did not think of them as a likely match. Michaud was a well-dressed and well-spoken woman while Daveggio did not pay much attention to his words or attire. He would dress up in worn-out clothes and biker boots as Michaud carried herself in a way that was completely different to her way of life. Her self-confidence was very evident in every interaction, which was a striking contrast to Daveggio's visible discomfort within a crowd.

Analysts and psychological experts say that, much like Daveggio, Michaud could also have been suffering from a multiple personality disorder. When amongst people, her ladylike, champagne-loving side would be prominent, but the underlying loud-mouthed and aggressive personality was always there. Later on, a few close friends of Michelle Michaud went on record to say that, despite her conservative dressing and sophisticated manner of speaking, she never shied away from describing her sex life in graphic detail.

As opposed to her open and outspoken verbal interactions, Daveggio was closed off and never talked about his sexual preferences in front of anyone. Whenever he was approached by a woman, he would quietly move away. It was assumed that his need to be in control was such that a woman making the first move on him turned him off.

After meeting Michaud, Daveggio could not help his attraction towards her. They may have been different in outward appearances and demeanor, but it can be said that ultimately they were cut from the same cloth. At thirty-seven years of age, Michaud was an attractive woman with an athletic body. Both her mind and appearance attracted Daveggio from the very beginning. She was an intelligent and sharp woman who exuded self-confidence as well as poise. Michaud would talk openly about her sexual desires and fantasies, often speaking about how she would like to interact with her partner. Evidently, Daveggio and Michaud connected over similar sexual preferences.

It was quite surreal that a well-dressed and well-spoken mother of two could spin such dark carnal fantasies that could leave the listener speechless.

Appearance-wise, there was no surprise that Michelle Michaud managed to make heads turn. With dark red hair and striking green eyes, she attracted men everywhere she went. Her family moved from one place to another before settling down in South Sacramento. Little is known about her early life, as contradicting accounts surfaced during the trial. According to some versions, her family appeared outwardly middle class and fairly normal, while others hinted towards disturbances and frequent misdemeanors.

However, all accounts stated that, beginning in her teens, Michaud started to rebel against her family and all figures of authority in her life. She dropped out of school at the age of fifteen and began a relationship with a boy who already was on the run from the law. Michaud soon began to experiment with drugs and forayed into prostitution. She ran away from home and bounced from one location to another before coming across James Daveggio in Bobby Joe's.

The twisted pair soon formed a fairly strong bond that led to Daveggio moving in with Michaud after just a short period of dating. Whilst Daveggio's interest in his partner began to fade gradually, Michaud did everything she could to keep them together. She even allowed him to fraternize with various other women and suffered physical abuse as well. Their terror spree which went from California to Nevada began soon after he was fired from his job at the bar. Daveggio turned Michaud's minivan into a torture chamber and raped several victims inside.

His partner was responsible for luring them in and occasionally participated during the act as well. It boggles the imagination of analysts and psychological experts everywhere as to what prompted Michaud to become a murderer and serial kidnapper. While she may have been booked for run-ins with law as a rebellious youngster, there was little which implied that she would go on to lead a life of full-blown crime. During her spree with Daveggio, she was arrested for the second time in her life for writing bad checks but was let out shortly. Once out of police custody, they started moving again, taking the van around and targeting innocent victims across various cities, even crossing state lines.

The relationship between the two has been the subject of many studies and books. Authors have tried their best to identify the dynamics that Daveggio and Michaud built upon. While the connection may have been inspired by twisted sexual fantasies, the murder element came in much later. Michaud may have known about her partner's violent nature and aggressive streak, choosing to adapt to his way of life. Soon enough, her sociopathic tendencies rose above and broke through the seemingly poised demeanor. In her reign of terror, along with Daveggio, she left behind a trail of scarred and traumatized victims.

During the trial, Michaud was also termed as

'pure evil' and many believed that the death penalty was the only appropriate justice. The heinous crimes for which both Daveggio and Michaud were responsible had left the whole country reeling in shock. It was presumed that the perpetrators felt little or no remorse for their crimes, as Michelle Michaud was known for openly boasting about their violent escapades and was constantly planning on upping the stakes in their criminal offences.

A witness called to the stand by Michaud's attorneys implied that her behavior was a reflection of the abuse and violence she might have suffered at the hands of various boyfriends early in her life. It was also claimed that her father may have raped her and thus prompted her decision to become a prostitute. Despite evidence of Michaud's father's innocence being presented in court, the defense continued to push for a psychological evaluation. However, at the end, justice prevailed and the federal jury handed out a death sentence to both Daveggio and Michaud.

Michelle Michaud has been a notorious criminal who will be remembered in the years to come. Many police officers and behavioral experts have conducted numerous studies and research on Michaud's background and history so as to come up with any explanation behind her erratic decline into the abyss of darkness. Some cite Daveggio's influence as a defining factor that led to Michaud becoming one-half of America's most vicious serial killer couple, while others say that the underlying dark side was already present and waiting to surface beyond the calm exterior. Her personality disorder was such that to passersby she seemed like a woman of great taste and striking looks. Michaud was well put together and at first glance was like any other native of California. There are accounts of her being hospitable and helpful on various occasions. According to one narrator, Michaud usually chose to stay away from sanctimonious people and was not a devout believer of any faith or religion; however, she did come to admire Father Kavanagh.

The priest gave numerous sermons and lessons at the church in Michaud's locality and somehow managed to make an impression on this rebellious girl. It was alleged that he became a prominent figure in her life and even watched over her on countless occasions. Apparently, her time with Father Kavanagh stayed a memory with her for a long time as she helped missionaries and church delegations that came by her house. It has been related that once a Mormon missionary group stopped at her house and were so impressed by Michaud's sincere and generous behavior that they offered her free painting services. While they painted her house, she prepared delicious meals as a token of appreciation for their free service.

The few accounts of Michelle Michaud's early days are all reminiscent of her rebellious days. She was always a free-spirited girl with little regard for rules and regulations, yet there was nothing so dark that could signify that the girl would go on to become one of the country's most hunted criminals. She had fairly good relations with a few family members and always had a number of friends despite the chip on her shoulder.

After dropping out of school, she had gone through a number of bad relationships that perhaps added to her erratic behavior and internal instability. The man she moved in with at the age of sixteen was a drug dealer and had been investigated by the police numerous times. Due to her relationship with him, Michaud began to experiment with hard drugs and ventured into dealing as well. Her first run-ins with the law occurred in 1991 when she was working at a massage parlor in Sacramento. The police raided the establishment that was supposedly a place for 'relaxation' but actually was covering a number of illegal activities from drug dealing to solicitation.

She was arrested along with other workers on the premises and released after serving a short sentence. Soon after her release, she changed locations and moved around constantly until Daveggio came into her life. This was a turning point in both of their lives, and they went on to become a deadly serial kidnapping and murdering duo who claimed the lives of several innocent women.

Spree of Terror

Analysts say that Daveggio was already a sociopath and his tendencies were fueled by Michael Ihde's influence. Michaud could have been propelled into joining the world of crime by her partner who was already bordering on psychopathic aggressiveness. Daveggio appeared like any other man to an onlooker but was masquerading his true nature beneath a slouchy and quiet demeanor. According to researchers and investigators, Daveggio was smiling slyly in his yearbook which could have been an early sign foreshadowing his perverse fantasies.

Michaud, on the other hand, was only involved in minor offences and prostitution before she met Daveggio at Bobby Joe's. Their relationship was twisted from the initial stage. While Daveggio managed the bar, Michaud was frequently heard relaying her dark and violent sexual fantasies to anyone who would listen. She would talk about her previous sexual encounters as well as anything she would like to do with her partner in the future. While outwardly, Michaud and Daveggio seemed polarities apart, they did have similar interests as far as sexual fantasies were concerned.

As their relationship progressed, things took a turn for the worse. Daveggio began to drift away and started taking multiple partners while Michaud held onto him, believing that if she let him live his way, he was going to come back to her. Soon enough, he was fired from the bar for his erratic behavior and constant fights with the customers. The couple's financial situation began to deteriorate, which was why they invited Daveggio's friend to sell drugs from their house. This was one occasion where luck did not side with the two; a police bust was carried out and all operations were halted.

Due to Daveggio's sex offender status, he was ordered to move away from the residence as there were children in the house. This was the time when his killer instincts began to completely take over his thought process. He began to take a keen interest in serial killers, especially Gerald Gallego. As the information came to light during the trial, Daveggio had already been charged with the rape of three women before the actual partnership was struck. He had been fined and arrested for soliciting a prostitute and offering alcohol to a minor girl. Prior to meeting Michaud, Daveggio had quite a rap sheet that included assault and various cases of abuse.

He was also using methamphetamines heavily and had a string of bad relationships. Michaud on the other hand was only arrested on accounts of prostitution before she met Daveggio, with her next conviction being for fraud after their relationship had begun.

After her partner was fired from his job,

Michaud became the sole breadwinner in the household. However, her business also took a severe hit when the drug abuse became a huge problem that prevented her from procuring clients. With so much less income to go on, the deadly team decided to explore possibilities. Daveggio, being greatly inspired by Gerald Gallego, tried to convince Michaud to join him in his evil plans just as Gerald did with his partner, Charlene. Analysts have stated that this was perhaps the point when something snapped inside Michelle Michaud.

Her brain was so addled by the drug abuse that rational thought no longer prevailed. Daveggio soon managed to convince her to lure over their first victim, her daughter's thirteen-year-old friend. The girl became the couple's first victim of rape but somehow escaped with her life. This was just the beginning of the pure terror that was going to be unleashed upon unsuspecting victims.

Community college student Alicia Paredes was walking home from a night class one evening when a green minivan stopped near her. She was abducted by the serial killing twosome and raped. Michaud and Daveggio let her go and did not kill her. Paredes reported the incident and worked with a sketch artist to get their sketched likenesses developed. However, luck was on the criminals' side, and they evaded any persecution or arrest for the time being. Paredes only caught the name 'Mickie' as she had heard the man calling out to the driver. Despite that detail, the police did not come up with any conclusive evidence of the crime or the perpetrators.

They went from one location to another, targeting victims and raping them. Somehow, the two managed to evade the police despite Michaud being arrested for a short period of time on account of bad checks due to her rising debt. Once she was out, the crime streak continued with Daveggio making several modifications inside the van, installing various tools that could be used to subdue the victims. The pair drove around Reno, Nevada, and took Juanita Rodriguez as their next victim. She was the one who put them on the map for investigating authorities in Reno.

While the couple released her after sexually assaulting her, they threatened her life if she ever told anyone about the incident. Terrified, Rodriguez went to the authorities and narrated her ordeal. During the incident, she had somehow managed to catch the mention of the name 'Mickie' vaguely. She passed on the information to the authorities who began to work on the case co-coordinating with the police in California where similar incidents had occurred. The name 'Mickie' had surfaced twice thus far, but there was no evidence of the perpetrator to whom it belonged. Both Daveggio and Michaud managed to evade any persecution or arrest and continued their crime spree without interruption.

They struck again soon after Rodriguez, this time in Sacramento. Seventeen-year-old Patty Wilson was the next victim who was tortured and raped. She was picked up by Michaud and lured into the minivan under the impression that they were going to experiment with some drugs together. After assaulting her, both Daveggio and Michaud contemplated killing her; however, she begged for her life and vowed to lie to the police about the incident. After driving around for a few hours, Wilson was let off with a threat that if she told the truth to anyone, she would be dead. The terrified girl knew that the couple was armed and very dangerous; they even knew where she lived.

When the authorities questioned her, Wilson made up a fake story and stuck to it despite the police suspecting fallacy. However, by this time, the authorities across Reno and California had enough to put together a case. Rodriguez had given a description of her male assailant, and the police had managed to come up with a sketch of the man. The woman driver could not be identified as the victim was unable to get a closer look at her. In a surprising twist of fate, it was Juanita Rodriguez who helped spur the chase of the serial raping and killing for the authorities. Michaud had not even imagined that Rodriguez would remember the details of her perpetrators. Although deeply traumatized, she relayed as much information as she could to the FBI investigators.

As the victims began to traverse across state lines, the Federal Bureau of Investigation was brought into the investigation. Special Agent Lynn J.

Ferrin immediately went to work, along with his team of detectives and criminalist Renee Romero. The criminalist was well versed in DNA samples and evidence checking, which is how he discovered that the male assailant who assaulted Rodriguez had either undergone a vasectomy or suffered from a medical condition.

While evidence collection was going on, Michaud and Daveggio struck again. This time the victim was a family member who also became a prime witness in the investigation later on. On November 18, 1997, a Sacramento police officer received a call that two girls had been molested and assaulted by a couple in a green minivan.

This was perhaps the beginning of the end for the serial killers. Baker revealed the names of the assailant and even confirmed that she heard Michaud admit to the rape of Juanita Rodriguez. The officer who took their statements looked up the names against previous charges and discovered that both Michaud and Daveggio had been arrested more than once. Upon further questioning, the whereabouts of the lethal pair remained unknown as they were living in their minivan and constantly moving from one place to another.

However, this was considered a major breakthrough in the case as the police now knew whom they were hunting for. Despite the efforts of the authorities and investigators, they could not prevent what was about to happen next.

The horror that unfolded on December 2, 1997, will go down as one of the worst setbacks in the progress of humanity. While Samson's murder led to an end of the three-month-long crime spree, it also reminded the people that there was an endless pit of darkness, which could have claimed any one of them. Vanessa Samson was a native of Pleasanton, California, where Daveggio had spent most of his adult life. The duo had returned to the town as it seemed target-rich around Thanksgiving. Parking their minivan near a high school, the serial killers went out looking for their next victim. Temporarily, they were forced to move away as a teacher caught them around campus and raised an alarm.

During this time, an arrest warrant was issued for both Michelle Michaud and James Daveggio in multiple cases of assault and rape. Yet the authorities closed in a little too late. They could not save Vanessa Samson's life as she became their next and final victim before they were arrested by the police.

The couple had become more and more erratic due to heavy drug abuse. They were making mistakes, which led the police toward closing in on them by the minute. As the chase was on, Daveggio decided that he could wait no longer to find the next victim. He sent Michaud on a lookout again and proceeded to purchase various tools that he would use to torture Samson before killing her.

While Vanessa Samson's murder is what led to justice being served, it was the information given by Rodriguez which led the authorities to two of the deadliest criminal's at the time. They not only raped several innocent victims, but as the case progressed and more details came forward it was revealed that their involvement in various other abductions and assaults was also possible. Speculation arose that both Michaud and Daveggio had been behind the disappearance of Jaycee Lee Dugard with a witness putting the former at the scene of the crime.

There were a few unsolved cases, which could well be closed if they were connected to the victims, and it looked very likely they had taken more victims than the ones who had come forward.

During their trial, it was established that the couple had raped and assaulted six known victims, all of them young girls. The crime spree was such that it spared no one who was deemed a suitable victim. As investigators delved into the details of each crime, they unraveled more horrors. It was evident that the pair was one of the deadliest criminal partnerships to have struck across the country.

Before Daveggio and Michaud, the Federal Bureau of Investigation had come across a similar couple who wreaked havoc within the same vicinity. The Sacramento and Nevada authorities could never forget Gerald and Charlene Gallego, both of whom were responsible for the sexual torture and murder of eleven girls. Daveggio had, in fact, been inspired by the serial rapist and killer. Studying Gallego's crime spree during the 1980s, the authorities found striking similarities between their victims and those of Michaud and Daveggio. Just as Gerald Gallego had convinced his partner Charlene to get on board with his gruesome and vicious plans, James Daveggio followed suit. He brought out the worst in Michaud, and her darker side eventually took over.

She joined her boyfriend on a long spree of torture, assault, rape and then murder. While the serial raping and killing couple drew comparisons with Gerald and Charlene Gallego on the basis of a similar mode of operation, they managed to leave their own mark on the criminal history of California and Nevada.

In the late 1970s, Gerald Gallego came across Charlene at a poker club in Sacramento and the two soon began to date. Both were into recreational drugs and did not shy away from a wild experience every now and then. After living together for a short span of time, Gallego began to find their sex life dull and monotonous. His partner did not excite him anymore and thus began his search for something more stimulating. Whether Charlene was aware of his sexual fantasies from before is unknown; however, the investigation did bring to light details of Gallego's violent sexual preferences.

Drugs played a very important role in the couple's lives and fueled Gallego's erratic behavior. When Charlene got pregnant, Gerald Gallego decided that it was time to put into play his twisted fantasies. He convinced his partner to lure over innocent young victims so that he could satisfy his raging desire. Both Charlene and Gallego would scout targets at various places such as malls and restaurants, after which the former would invite them in under false pretenses. They too operated out of a van where Gerald Gallego would torture and assault his victims.

Their murderous crime spree claimed the lives of eleven innocent girls, who were also subjected to sexual slavery. After raping and murdering two teenagers in California, Gerald Gallego found himself being pursued by authorities as their bodies were discovered at a farm where he had been seen by a witness. Soon afterwards, Gallego's daughter also came forward with a molestation claim against her father. While an arrest warrant was issued for him, the police did not find the murderous two till after they had left a trail of eight more victims in their wake. They constantly were bouncing from one place to another, which made it difficult for the authorities to track them down in the 1980s.

Finally, Gallego and Charlene fled to Reno, Nevada, and married under an alias. 1984 was the year which saw the deadly killing duo caught and convicted after claiming numerous victims in California and Nevada. After their trial, Gerald Gallego was sentenced to death for the atrocities committed while his partner Charlene was awarded prison time. The jury determined that, in light of all the facts and evidence, the woman had been a mere pawn in Gallego's evil schemes and had not actually participated in the torture or sexual acts. Hence, she was handed out a sentence for sixteen years and eight months in a Nevada prison.

Analysts and investigators found that, when it came to choosing their victims and torturing them, James Anthony Daveggio and Michelle Michaud mirrored Gallego and Charlene. The serial raping and killing of Daveggio and Michaud went after unsuspecting young girls from California and Nevada. While they only murdered their last victim, the assault and physical torture inflicted upon the other girls was very similar to Gallego's method.

Despite that, James Daveggio and Michelle Michaud could not have been more different than Gerald and Charlene Gallego when it came to relationship dynamics. Most psychological experts were of the opinion that Michaud was the dominant one in the partnership. Whilst Charlene had played the role of a bystanding accomplice, Michelle was an equal partner in every sexual assault which had been carried out.

According to a statement made by the investigating officials from the Federal Bureau of Investigation (FBI) later on, it was the 'first of its kind' case where a woman partner had "allegedly taken an equal role in a series of sexual assaults." Charlene Gallego was merely an 'enabler' but not Michelle Michaud, who could never be pushed into the background by a man. Daveggio and Michaud's seventeen-year-old victim Patty Wilson somehow confirmed that when she was lured into the van and captured; her assailant was, in fact, Michaud and not Daveggio since he could not perform at the time.

Further details surfaced and revealed that Michaud was the one who threatened all their victims before letting them go. She would warn them not to go 'somewhere alone' because they wouldn't be 'so lucky again' the next time. The young girls would be absolutely terrified and would refrain from even telling anyone the details of the incident. It was already established that Daveggio and Michaud carried a weapon with them, which had been witnessed by both Patty Wilson and Juanita Rodriguez.

The other victims also knew that they were armed and could kill them at any time, which is why the young women usually complied with their acts of atrocities. Juanita Rodriguez recounted the ordeal to the authorities later on, and her sheer terror was evident in each detail. Unfortunately, this was one thing that she could never erase from her mind. The incident had to be retold quite a few times: to the medical staff at the hospital who examined her with a standard rape kit procedure to gather evidence, then to the detectives, as well as the federal authorities. Rodriguez had to relive the horrors of that night more than once, and that thought alone was enough to send shivers down everyone's spine.

However, despite the terrible ordeal she went through, Juanita Rodriguez's bravery was what led to them being eventually captured. Detective Desiree Carrington of Placer County was key to closing this case. After meeting Rodriguez, she knew immediately that they were not going to stop at one victim and that the police department had another Gallego-like case on their hands. Carrington was very understanding and sympathetic towards Rodriguez's ordeal, but she knew that no matter how traumatic the rape incident, every minute detail had to be collected. Preserving any sense of modesty on the victim's part would only hurt their investigation and allow the man and woman to roam free.

Carrington, her partner Bill Summers and FBI agents immediately went to work around the area looking for any evidence or suspicious people. The investigating teams knew that time was of the essence as they realized the pair could strike anywhere and at any time. Special Agent Lynn J. Ferrin, who had come across a lot of these cases during his long career in law enforcement, recognized that solving the case was not going to be an easy task. After hearing about the rape incident, Agent Ferrin had wasted no time in contacting Juanita Rodriguez and conducting an extensive interview with her.

Rodriguez told him that the couple had several personal items and sleeping bags stashed away in their van. This was one factor that worried Agent Ferrin somewhat as he realized that not having a permanent address made it all the more challenging for the authorities to track down the assailants. The couple were on the move constantly and could be anywhere across state lines. However, the agent was very well trained in handling violent crimes, particularly Title 18 offences that focus on abductions and sexual abuse. He knew that he would have to inspect every nook and cranny to find this deadly couple.

Juanita Rodriguez revealed that whilst she was desperately trying to keep herself alive, she attempted to engage the couple in conversation to gain their sympathy. She said that the man had a fondness for one particular Johnny Cash song. When she asked what it was based upon, his reply chilled her to the bone. Her male assailant described the song as being one about a man who shot and killed a man from Reno just so he could 'watch him die.' Rodriguez instantly knew that she could meet a similar fate if she didn't do something fast.

She made up a story and lied that her nine month old baby would be alone in the world if she was killed. Somehow, the woman assailant took mercy upon her and decided to let her go. Rodriguez was warned not to turn around and to keep walking for twenty minutes. Analysts and investigating authorities assessed from the details she revealed that Michelle Michaud was the dominant figure in the couple's relationship. Juanita Rodriguez had stated that when the man got tired of abusing her, he seemed almost remorseful but was very clear that he did not mean to 'take her back' as she might 'do something stupid.' However, after she kept on begging and promising that she wouldn't, he turned to the woman driver to ask what they should do with their victim; surprisingly, she said that they should 'let her go.'

Similar to Rodriguez's ordeal was Patty Wilson's night of horror. She had been lured into the van by Michaud under the pretense of doing a 'line of meth' together. Wilson was already familiar with the man and woman as she had seen them around the area quite a few times. However, what followed was something that she could not have imagined even in her most fearful nightmare.

As soon as she entered the green minivan, Wilson was punched by Daveggio and knocked out cold. Much later, she recalled the physical impact of the hit, which caused her to 'see stars' and pass out for almost five minutes. While the perpetrators subjected Wilson to assault, the male assailant could not perform sexually and backed out of raping her. The terrified girl recounted that she had told Daveggio how the entire ordeal was reminiscent of her stepfather's abuse. Apparently, this killed the man's mood and he moved away. However, Wilson still had much more to endure. The man called out to the woman, who wanted 'her turn' since he wanted nothing to do with her anymore. Hence, the girl was subjected to rape at the hands of the woman driver after she parked the minivan in the hills near Livermore, which is a town close to Pleasanton, California.

By the end of the ordeal, Wilson was almost convinced that she was going to die. The couple had stated that they could not drop her back to where she worked as it could be risky. They did not want to end up in jail.

She begged them to let her go and promised that she would lie to her manager, making up a false story as to what happened. Wilson told them that her manager would call the authorities as she was not the kind of person to take off from work like that, and when the police came, she would lie to them as well.

The couple drove around contemplating what to do and finally decided that they would let her go. However, the false story came from them. Wilson was told that after she went back, she would say that three teenage boys kidnapped her from the parking lot of the gaming arcade where she worked. She also had to elaborate that the boys raped her at the hills and then dropped her off. Patty Wilson agreed to everything and in return was let off at a gas station situated on Dublin Boulevard. She called the manager from the gas station and repeated the exact same story about being raped by three teenage boys.

While her manager believed the fake story, the Dublin police who had been informed of the incident found it greatly distorted. They were skeptical about its authenticity but did not manage to get anything further from seventeen-year-old Patty Wilson. The girl was well aware that her assailants were deadly; she had seen a gun in the passenger seat as well. She knew that the couple had her residence details and could kill her at any time if she revealed any mention of them.

There was no doubt in her or the authorities' minds that this was a dangerous, armed, and out-of-control pair of serial rapists. Nobody in their path was safe, and until they were caught, everything had to be done to keep the victims safe.

The Events of December 2, 1997

Much has been said and written about the events leading up to and on December 2, 1997. This was when finally they claimed the life of an innocent 22-year-old girl, Vanessa Lei Samson. The horrors are such that neither the authorities and nor the victim's family and friends will ever be able to suppress the incident's memory. This was the time when investigating officials and the police were already closing in on the two. Their crime spree had continued across the states of Nevada and California, but the authorities were now finally on the trail of the suspects.

Vanessa Lei Samson

An arrest warrant had been issued for both Michaud and Daveggio. From September to

December, the deadly couple had taken five known victims, and Vanessa would be their sixth.

It was as if nothing mattered anymore. All hell had broken loose.

Vanessa Lei Samson was a lively and cheerful young girl who still lived with her family and was close to all her siblings. She was studying at the Ohlone College and saving up for further tuition. Her hopes and dreams were brutally snatched away from her as she became James Daveggio and Michelle Michaud's latest victim. However, unlike the prior ones, Samson was not lucky enough to escape with her life.

By picking out Vanessa Samson, the couple changed from their usual victimization. They did not abduct her from a dark alley or in the night from a far-fetched place. Surprisingly enough, her kidnapping occurred in the morning hours and within a fairly populated area.

James Anthony Daveggio and Michelle Michaud were on the lookout for a new victim. Later, in the trial, it was revealed that the sadistic couple termed their excursions as 'hunts' and 'adventures.' Michaud described the rapes and torture inflicted upon each victim as an 'adventure,' while Daveggio chose to refer to the escapades as 'huntings.' It was evident that they both found it quite thrilling.

The couple had been scouting the grounds of a high school in Pleasanton, California, when a teacher found their presence suspicious and they were forced to move away. It was presumed that they chose such places as they were target-rich and young girls could be easily picked up without raising any alarm. By an unfortunate twist of fate, Vanessa Samson showed up on their radar, and what followed was one of the most brutally executed crimes in the history of the United States.

People who are familiar with the area of Pleasanton, California, describe it as being a relatively safe and close-knit community where previously such crimes were unheard of. The Samsons were like any other typical all-American family, enjoying a quiet life in the suburbs. It was Thanksgiving time, and the family had all gathered together to celebrate the occasion. The mother, Christina Samson, was overjoyed that all of her family had come together to spend time.

Her children, Vanessa, Nicole and Vincent, along with her husband, Daniel, would finally be able to get away from all the hassle of work, study and other activities for a short while. It was going to be a good, relaxing vacation for the Samson family. However, things took a turn for the worse just a few days after the holidays ended. Unknown to the family, they were already in town and had claimed an innocent victim in an area not far away from where they lived.

Just a week prior to Vanessa Samson's murder, the couple, who had checked into a motel, abducted and assaulted a young teenage girl. The victim later recalled that both Michelle Michaud and James Daveggio had stated something along the lines of attacking another girl next. She admitted that Daveggio had raped her and then let her go. However, she had heard him saying that the holidays would make up for the biggest 'shopping days of the entire year and would be best for killing somebody.' The authorities discovered that, just a few days later, the pair were on the hunt for their next victim.

This one would not be so lucky. The couple drove around various markets and went to Hayward Kmart where they purchased curling irons and duct tape. Their van, which also served as a torture chamber, was fitted with ropes and other tools that were used to subdue the victims. Michelle Michaud and James Daveggio took their purchases to a Motel 6, situated in Pleasanton, and checked into Room 137. On November 30, 1997, they were spotted outside the motel with Michelle Michaud's green minivan being parked outside.

The police who were rushing against time to catch the serial raping and killing couple revealed that they stayed close to Foothill High School where it was easy to scout potential victims. On the very same day, Daveggio and Michaud were also caught on tapes within an adult toy shop. They made various purchases, including a cassette of a pornographic video titled 'Submissive Young Girls.'

On the fateful day of December 2, 1997,

Vanessa Samson was about to go to her job she had landed just a few weeks before. At 7:30 in the morning, she stepped out with her lunch and backpack, bidding farewell to her mother. Samson was already used to walking short distances and did not mind the walk from her home to the offices of SCJ Insurance Services. Her sister, Nicole, was staying with a friend and had offered her a ride to work that day; however, she had not responded back so Samson had chosen to walk.

It seemed as if nothing was going right for her that day. An unsuspecting Samson walked on Singleton Street and then onto the road that would intersect Kern and Page courts, leading her to Gibraltar Drive. This was when she heard the wheels of a van crunching past her. For about a minute, Samson did not pay any attention to the green minivan until it turned around and stopped right in front of her. A man stepped out and dragged her inside.

Roofers working at a nearby house heard a loud and desperate scream, which was quickly muffled. A green minivan was also spotted driving away.

What happened with Vanessa Samson includes gruesome details of torture and continuous abuse, after which, despite being told that she would be let off, she was brutally murdered. As it was revealed later, Samson was strangled by a rope and her body dumped near an embankment. Her body was discovered half-frozen a couple days later, by which time the two had already been apprehended, but their involvement in her murder was unknown.

The police had caught the couple at their motel and arrested them on charges of assault and abuse. However, since the whereabouts of Vanessa Samson were still unknown, the truth about her murder was yet to surface.

According to case details, it was revealed that Vanessa Samson had been tied with a rope and repeatedly assaulted for almost half a day. She had been tortured with the cords of the curling irons and other tools that the couple had in their minivan. After the assault in the van, they brought their victim to the Sundowner Motel at South Lake Tahoe. They checked into Room 5, and nobody spotted anything suspicious. It was revealed that this was the motel where Samson's abuse and torture carried on for long hours.

She may have been told that she could go free when the couple took her along Highway 88, but the brutality knew no end. Samson was strangled with a rope and her body was dumped in the snow on an embankment. The police later found it in such a terrible condition that nobody would be able to forget it for years to come.

Vanessa Samson was a girl who was loved and adored by one and all. Her family and friends were in a frenzied state of panic when she failed to report to work and return home. Her coworker knew that it was not at all like Samson, who had hardly ever been late to her job, to not show up at all. She immediately informed the family who began a search for their beloved family member.

Her friends and family called up every known acquaintance and hospital in the area but could not obtain any knowledge of her safety. The last anybody had seen of Vanessa was her walking out the door for work. Christina Samson had a horrible 'sinking' feeling in her stomach, yet she hoped and prayed for the best. Her mother wanted to believe that she might have gone to visit her close friend, Raul Guilliarte in Davis; he was supposed to come down during the holidays but had not been able to make it. However, all her hopes were shattered when Guilliarte revealed that he had neither heard from nor seen Vanessa Samson.

As time passed, Samson's friends and family became increasingly disturbed. They were almost certain that something terrible had happened to her. Vincent, Samson's brother, took off from his job in San Francisco and organized a search party for his sister. He even took help from the authorities and had fliers posted. Yet all of this was to no avail. Vanessa Samson had been dead for many hours, and her body was lying cold in a nearby area.

Vincent Samson felt directly responsible for his sister's disappearance and wanted to do everything that he could to find her. As the details were revealed later, he believed that he had failed his sister at the time. Despite everyone's best efforts in finding Vanessa Samson's trail, nothing could be turned up. Her assailants were already in police custody and charged with rape and assault. However, Samson's death was still not linked to them.

On December 4, 1997, Vanessa Samson's body was discovered and the police began investigating. Along the way, it began to look like the murder could be connected to the pair. They had been examining the objects in the couple's minivan, and things were getting more suspicious with each discovery. As the police and investigators stripped down the van, they found various tools of torture, a few of which had blood on them that looked fairly fresh. Vanessa Samson had already been missing for two days, and it was looking more like a certainty that these two were directly involved in her kidnapping.

After her body was discovered, the police and investigating officials found evidence that indicated that she was murdered by one or both of the killers. Vincent Samson was the first to be notified of his sister's unfortunate demise. A trucker had spotted the body at 10:45 a.m. on that fateful day, and later on Vincent Samson was the one who had to break the news to his family. He told the police that all that was going through his mind at the time was he will have to deliver such news to his family, which was going to alter their lives in every possible way.

When he arrived home, his mother, Christina Samson, instantly knew that something was wrong. Her daughter had been 'taken away' and nothing was going to be the same again.

Later on, during the investigation, she said that 'a part of her died' that day, and she was going to cry over it for the rest of her life. Her precious daughter, who had held so much promise, was taken away brutally and made to suffer immensely due to no fault of her own. Vanessa Samson had only been the 'pretty girl with black hair' who suddenly caught the eye of the burly, bearded man with several tattoos. Daveggio then made his partner turn around, pick her up and force her into the van. The only mistake that the unsuspecting girl had made that day was to walk to work.

The Investigation and Arrest

After brutally torturing and assaulting Vanessa Samson, James Anthony Daveggio and Michelle Lyn Michaud drove around Highway 88, possibly looking for a dumping ground. They settled on an embankment and, after tying and gagging her, Daveggio strangled her with a black nylon rope that the couple had purchased a few days before. Before selecting Vanessa Samson as their next victim, the two had already decided that they were going to take it up a notch in their crime spree.

The police were hot on their heels and closing in, while drugs and methamphetamines were spurring their erratic behavior more so than ever before. Their green Dodge Caravan had been spotted in the parking lot of the Motel 6 in Pleasanton; hence, it was only a matter of time before someone reported it.

Despite the investigating authorities being so close, they could not manage to save Vanessa Samson's life. There was perhaps a chance that the couple may have escaped the police for a longer time, even after murdering Samson. However, a mistake on Michaud's part was all it took for the police and detectives to corner them and take them in. Michelle Michaud was due for a court hearing in Sacramento on account of her being indicted for writing bad checks. She was supposedly going to meet her mother on the way as well.

On December 2, 1997, just a few hours after Vanessa Samson's murder, Michelle Michaud made the grave error of stopping to collect her welfare check. She also made a trip to a check cashing store and was instantly spotted by the local police. While she continued on her way to South Lake Tahoe, where her hearing was scheduled at a nearby court, the authorities were informed immediately.

The police followed the trail to Lakeside Inn, situated within Stateline, Nevada. Officers had questioned her mother, who also gave up her daughter's whereabouts, and they were able to pinpoint a location. A young girl had also come forward with the information that she had been the couple's victim in a minivan that was very similar to the one parked outside the motel's casino. Special Agent Ferrin led the hunt, ordering all the police officials to spread out and cover as much ground as possible. The parking area, restaurant and casino were all swept thoroughly and, within minutes, the police arrested Michelle Lyn Michaud from Room 133.

James Anthony Daveggio was playing slots at the casino and was instantly handcuffed and taken away as well. They were charged with assaults and kidnappings at the time, pending a trial which sentenced them for these crimes in 1999. The police were definitely relieved that after a month-long chase, they had finally caught these two monsters who had been terrorizing people across California and Nevada.

Yet more horrors were about to unfold. As the investigating team examined the van and each piece of evidence in detail, they discovered a few objects that were indicating something sinister. The authorities had already started to investigate any possible links to the couple and Vanessa Samson's murder. It turned out that Michelle Michaud, who was being held in Douglas County Jail, saw the news about the 22-year-old's body being discovered off Highway 88, and she blurted out to a friend of hers in prison that they might be responsible for it.

The authorities immediately began to question her further until she waived her rights and started answering their questions. During her interviews, she mentioned Vanessa Samson quite a few times and appeared to trail off while recalling some of the details of her kidnapping. Her behavior indicated that she was involved in Samson's kidnapping and definitely a murder suspect. The authorities spurred their investigation further and tried to find evidence which could possibly connect the two to Samson's abduction. The team soon came across the gags, bloodied ropes and white towels, evidence of a struggle.

They questioned Michaud again and she revealed that one of the gags had Samson's saliva on it as neither she nor her partner had wiped it off. The police soon found it along with a curling iron that had a severed cord and duct tape. Everything was sent to the laboratories for testing, and the results shocked everyone.

The curling iron was bloody and contained other bodily excretions as well. It was revealed that the tape also carried Michelle Lyn Michaud's right thumbprint. There was obviously no doubt in anyone's mind that they had made the authorities' worst fears come true and claimed the life of an innocent victim.

Vanessa Samson's murder was what led to the couple being handed out a death sentence. Their act was referred to as 'demonic' and 'vicious' with Vincent Samson openly addressing James Daveggio and Michelle Michaud in court and referring to them both as nothing but evil. There was no doubt that the death penalty was justice served and this twisted couple deserved nothing less.

Police and investigating officials were astounded by the gruesome details as they came to light, with some even stating that the notorious couple was a 'match made in hell.' Daveggio and Michaud had inflicted torture and abuse on all of their victims, going to another level of extreme with Vanessa Samson. While they had managed to evade the police on countless occasions, Pleasanton, California, was the end of their crime spree.

The police across Nevada and California began to search for the couple after identifying them. Investigating officials had already started building a case against a male-female team of attackers in Reno when Juanita Rodriguez reported her rape and assault at the Placer County Sheriff's Department. While the sketches were somewhat hazy, the police across the two states were on alert and looking out for any such suspicious couple. At the time, luck somehow sided with Daveggio and Michaud, and they managed to keep themselves out of sight.

After hearing the victims' accounts, the police hastened in their efforts to catch the rapists. The law enforcement agencies had seen first-hand the carnage that the two had left behind. It now became even more certain that this couple was unhinged and capable of the worst.

Investigating officials finally tracked down

the couple and cornered them in Pleasanton, California. At that time, the charges against them consisted of assault and rape. When Vanessa Samson's body was discovered, the police began to search for the perpetrators. This was when the Daveggio and Michaud case became a murder investigation. While the former's mate had brought the information regarding her involvement in the murder, it wasn't until two days later that the evidence proved what everybody had already assumed. The news report had mentioned that the murder weapon was a black nylon rope. Michaud saw this and started to fear that she was going to be implicated once the police found conclusive proof.

After long, intensive interviews, the officers managed to put together a clear picture. The woman had claimed that there was some evidence of the murder on a few tools and torture objects found in the van. As it turns out, she was right. James Daveggio was also questioned and it was learned that he had indeed repeatedly assaulted and then murdered Vanessa Samson by strangling her. While Michaud later contested her statements, the jury and court held fast to her testimony and even brought it to Daveggio's trial.

She was sentenced to death for murder and found guilty on all counts of rape and assault. Her partner met the same fate, and eventually, the twisted two were separated from each other. Michaud was transferred to federal custody and assigned attorneys.

Eventually, the two were handed over to Alameda County where a grand jury indicted them for the abduction and brutal murder of 22-year-old Vanessa Samson. During the course of their trials in 1999, they were also handed out sentences for assaults and rapes across Nevada and California.

Perhaps their sentencing gave closure to their victims who had been waiting for justice to be served. The terrified girls who had been afraid to come forward mustered the courage to open up about their suffering to the authorities. Some of their victims testified in front of the jurors at the trial. Patty Wilson, who had been scared into silence until their arrest, finally made her story public. She revealed the atrocities committed against her when the couple kidnapped her from the parking lot and then later threatened her to force her to lie.

As further evidence surfaced, it was claimed that Daveggio, who was already a registered sex offender prior to meeting Michaud, might have been involved in a few other rapes and killings before going on the crime spree with his partner.

Trial and Further Details

The arrest of Michelle Michaud and James Daveggio may have brought peace of mind to the authorities, but there was a lot more still to come. Vanessa Samson, who had been reported missing for two days, was found dead with visible marks of abuse and torture. Once it was proven that they were behind her murder and assault, their five-year-long tedious trial began. The death sentence was justly handed out, and the family of the victim had some satisfaction in that the killers of their beloved family member got what they deserved.

However, during the trial, there was nothing but pain and difficulty for not just Vanessa Samson's family but also the couple's numerous rape victims. The girls who had suffered abuse at the hands of Daveggio and Michaud had to recount the horrific details of their ordeal and relive it. Meanwhile, Samson's family and friends had to sit through the court proceedings which focused on the torture and abuse that the girl had to endure before she was killed so brutally.

Christina Samson and her husband stated that they would forever be 'haunted' by what happened to their little girl. The mother also said that she was going to mourn her daughter's death every day as her suffering was so great that it could never let her live in peace. Vanessa 'Ness' Samson was 'defenseless and alone' as well as 'frightened beyond words.' During the court proceedings, Vincent Samson addressed James Anthony Daveggio and placed a framed picture of his sister beside him.

He reminisced about his sister right from her childhood days, remembering the times he used to pay her to wrap Christmas presents. Vincent Samson also recalled the beautiful and responsible adult she had grown up to be, caring for everyone and never backing out of a commitment. All of Vanessa Samson's family and friends jam-packed the courtroom while the trial lasted, and they always showed up wearing purple ribbons to commemorate Vanessa Samson's memory as it was her favorite color.

Vincent Samson also questioned Daveggio, stating that what could he possibly say to a person who 'raped, molested and killed' his younger sister. He referred to him as a 'demon' who had committed 'vile' acts against innocent children.

The brother of Vanessa Samson was not the only man referring to the monsters as vicious and vile in open court. Alameda County Superior Judge Larry Goodman, who handed out the death penalty sentence, also referred to the incident of Vanessa Samson's murder and brutal torture as 'cruel, senseless, vicious, and depraved.' He stated that the death penalty was indeed appropriate for the heinous crimes for which they were responsible.

On the day of the sentencing, the dark and morbid tale of the slaying and torture was narrated by the jurors one last time. Just before the proceedings began, Vincent Samson expressed his confidence that 'justice was going to be served.'

While recounting the details of the murder, Alameda County Senior Deputy District Attorney Angela Backers stated that the duo had 'promised' Samson that they were going to let her go just like the victims prior to her. However, after driving around the area, they decided upon a murder site and eventually strangled her with a six-foot-long nylon rope.

The District Attorney told the jury, comprised of five men and seven women, that Vanessa Samson's murder capped the couple's six-victim spree that had spanned over a couple of months. They had subjected young innocent girls to abuse and sexual assault, not even leaving their own daughters unharmed. Backers presented the discovered evidence in court that included the pornographic video from the adult shop, a book about serial killers entitled 'The Dead of Night,' bloodied curling irons with Michaud's fingerprints on the duct tape, and a pack of serial killer cards. She stated that the couple was mostly inspired by the Gallegos with the cards featuring both Gerald and Charlene prominently.

Their rape and abuse of victims followed a similar pattern to the notorious criminal serial killing and rapist couples of the 1980s. Backers further said that the couple had probably upped the stakes and progressed to murder as they also aspired to have their pictures immortalized in serial killer cards, just like the Gallegos.

The initial arrest was made in the case of Juanita Rodriguez's assault in Reno, where Michaud pleaded guilty and was sentenced to fifteen years, while Daveggio was handed a twenty-five-year sentence.

The District Attorney added murder to the charges, thereby convincing the jury to recommend a death penalty.

Michaud initially contested the terms of her sentence, but the court dismissed all such objections and proceeded as scheduled. The forty-three-year-old and her lover were being investigated jointly by the Federal Bureau of Investigation and Placer County Sheriff's Department for assault and kidnapping. The police officials tracked them down to a motel in Stateline, Nevada, and isolated the two, arresting them on the premises.

In a twist of irony, the Sheriff's Department had secured the arrest warrant on the very day Vanessa Samson was abducted and murdered, December 2, 1997. When Special Agent Ferrin ordered his team to secure the area and lock the place down, he strategically planned the arrest. Michaud claimed in her appeal that her arrest had been on unlawful grounds and hence she was challenging her conviction.

One of the agents in the team was sent up to Michaud's room, claiming to be the hotel manager and asking her to come outside as her boyfriend needed assistance. This was a way to bring Michelle Michaud out and arrest her. In reality, James Daveggio had already been found at the slots and taken into police custody. Soon after, his partner also met the same fate. Once Michaud was surrounded by the law enforcement officials, she was quietly apprehended and taken into another hotel room where the agent cuffed her to the chair.

Special Agent Ferrin got Michaud to sign consent forms for searching their vehicle and read out the Miranda rights to her. She waived them and was sent into an interview room where FBI agents and Place County Detectives were waiting to question her. However, once in the room, she asked for the bathroom, immediately halting the interview. Michaud was booked into the Douglas County jail in Nevada on counts of possession and hardcore usage of controlled substances. Meanwhile the police searched inside the Dodge Caravan and came up with more evidence of suspicious activity.

Based on that, a warrant was issued for Michelle Michaud on charges of aiding, abetting and kidnapping. Just a day after the discovery of Vanessa Samson's body, Michaud saw a police report which implied that, upon investigating, the authorities had been able to narrow down the suspected murderers.

After seeing that, Michaud was in the cell with Teresa Agoroastos, her mate, and became increasingly disturbed that she was going to be in so much 'trouble.'

The cellmate contacted Deputy Douglas Conrad and asked him to come over and talk to Michaud. He ordered the women to come to the front of their dorm, after which Teresa Agoroastos revealed that Michaud had information regarding a murder. While the distraught woman remained silent and neither confirmed nor denied her mate's statement, Conrad took the matter further and informed his supervisor, Sergeant Arnie Digerud. Upon his instructions, Conrad took Michaud into a holding cell and waited for Sergeant Timothy Minister and FBI Agent Christopher Campion to interview the woman.

Agent Campion turned on the recorder and asked Michaud if she was aware of what was happening. He questioned whether she really did want to talk to him about a murder which had been bothering her and whether she would like to have an attorney present. After hearing her Miranda rights, she again waived them and submitted to further questioning. The interview lasted around nine to ten hours. Campion returned with Placer County Detective Desiree Carrington who had pursued the case relentlessly and made the arrest in her jurisdiction. After two more days of interviewing, Michaud was handed over to federal custody and prosecuted accordingly.

She was charged with kidnapping and transportation of the victims across state lines into Reno. Michaud raised objections to her conviction, but the appeal was rejected by the courts and her sentence was upheld.

Once again, she argued that her arrest had been unlawful due to incriminating circumstances. She stated in her appeal that the agents who had asked her to open the door of her hotel room violated her Fourth Amendment Rights. Her argument also covered the investigation in the Placer County jail. She said that her distressed state of mind blurred out any objectivity and she may have made the wrong statements.

The court rejected all of her arguments and stated that the ruse employed by the police to get her to come outside was justified as an arrest warrant had already been issued. While as far as those statements were concerned, the details were not clear and led to a murder investigation, at that point the circumstances had changed.

Both Michaud and Daveggio were separately arrested and taken into custody individually. As the court proceedings began, the twosome did not cross paths again. Michaud's testimony was used in Daveggio's trial but, other than that, it was the end for the murderous demons.

The investigating officials were unable to comprehend how two twisted individuals had managed to evade the authorities for so long. Their spree was heavily influenced by drugs, lust and an out-of-control rage on the part of Daveggio. It was by pure luck that they escaped arrest and managed to claim several victims in their wake.

Authorities across Nevada and California had been on the lookout for a couple in a green minivan but, despite numerous attempts, had failed to capture them. Ultimately, their arrest came after the murder of Vanessa Samson who had to give up her life for the couple to end their reign of terror. As the court proceedings revealed, the meeting of these two evolved into something very dangerous.

Michaud was a high-level prostitute, while Daveggio was a recognized sex offender who also worked with a gang. There was nothing good that could come out of their union. Nobody really knew what attracted them to each other. Michaud, from an early age, was the kind of individual who defied all social norms and went after what she wanted. The confident redhead was the kind of woman who was rarely turned down.

After getting together with Daveggio, she realized that he was highly unstable and she would not hold his interest for long unless she gave in to the abuse and his outrageous demands. Soon enough, she became the torturous, murdering woman who was handed down a death penalty. It was as if every moral fiber in her was compromised by the overwhelming desire to keep her partner pleased. It progressed to a stage where she initiated and actively participated in the abuse.

Psychologists believed that Michaud definitely liked assaulting and raping the innocent victims. The sexual motivation is actually a huge factor which kept the couple going from one place to another, scouting for victims and then subjecting them to physical and mental trauma.

James Daveggio, on the other hand, was a sociopathic disturbed individual since a young age. His past girlfriends and wives claimed that their loved ones had warned them about Daveggio's volatile temperament. Throughout adulthood, Daveggio had been involved in various incidents which indicated that a life of crime awaited him farther down the road. Despite receiving several warnings from the police officers, Daveggio did little to find an alternate path. He was absolutely convinced that darkness was his destiny and nothing could change that.

His firing from the job and removal from the gang, The Devil's Horsemen, gave him plenty of time to obsess over the twisted sexual perversions he carried around. He brought Michaud in as a partner on his journey of crime, convincing her that they could become the next Gerald and Charlene Gallego.

Regardless of their background and life experiences, nothing could justify the offenses for which they were proved responsible. Their respective attorneys may have argued for a lighter sentence and tried to defend the criminals, but it was evident that the only suitable justice would be capital punishment. When a witness brought in by Michaud's attorneys claimed that she had been abused and traumatized as a young girl, the state argued that this couldn't possibly be true as her father had been a military man with a strong character. Michaud had moved with her family like every other family in the forces from one place to another, settling down in a middle class neighborhood in California.

It was alleged that, despite gaining stability in her family life, she was getting restless. Michaud wanted to keep moving and, in order to do so, she made the decision to quit high school. The teenager then somehow forayed into prostitution. It was presumed that as a young girl with striking good looks, Michaud was aware of the effect she had on men. She also believed herself to be of a higher intelligence and astute observation, which is why her outlook on everyone around her was dismissive. According to Michaud, she did not want to be around such 'immature' people.

Psychologists and analysts examined the relationship between Daveggio and Michaud very closely. Once all the case facts and victims' testimonies came to light, it started to become clear that, whilst starting out, Daveggio was the one calling the shots, his partner quickly took over.

The notorious couple was compared constantly to Gerald and Charlene Gallego, who had even subjugated their victims into being 'sex slaves.' It was Charlene who was responsible for choosing the victims and luring them over to the van where Gerald Gallego would be waiting with a weapon. However, that remained the only common aspect between the two serial raping pairs.

After the Gallegos were caught, the case evidence which was presented implied that Charlene was not an active participant in either raping or assaulting the victims. In this case, there was Michelle Michaud who didn't back away from torturing or holding the victims down in all of the rapes, abductions, and then murder as well. There were instances when she chose the victims, lured them over and assaulted them subsequently. The authorities noted that this was a one-of-a-kind case where the female in a serial killer relationship was as much responsible for the abuse as her male counterpart.

Analysts concluded that, considering her personality from the beginning, it was no surprise that Michelle Michaud turned out to be the ruthless killer that she was. Since she was a teenager, Michaud had become heavily dependent on hardcore drugs, including methamphetamines, and was often under their influence. Her experience with various men had taught the woman how to hold her own. Unlike her partner at the time, Michaud managed to keep the inner turmoil subdued for as long as she could. Her outward appearance did not from any angle give away her profession or hint toward the instability she harbored.

When she and James Anthony Daveggio became romantically involved, they seemed like an odd pairing. While in the beginning, Daveggio might have been the 'bad' influence in her life, at the end, it was clear that Michaud had been enabling her own dark side all along. She dominated the relationship, taking over the acts of torture and making moves that previously were unheard of by a female perpetrator.

It also became evident that she had no remorse for any of her crimes. During the court proceedings, James Daveggio was asked by Vincent Samson, the victim's brother, if he had felt any guilt or remorse over his act. The grieving brother questioned Daveggio about the murder and whether he felt apologetic for the committed crimes. Vincent Samson did the same thing during Michaud's hearing.

The court allowed James Anthony Daveggio to respond to Vincent Samson just before he was to be sentenced. The forty-one-year-old, who was wearing the bright red jail attire, turned and faced the family of his unfortunate victim. He stated, "I, in fact, did not kill Ms. Samson. By law I am as guilty of her death as Michelle is." Daveggio went on further to say observing Vanessa Samson's family and realizing the love they had for her made him feel horrible about what he had done.

He looked at the 22-year-old's friends and

family and admitted that he 'had never seen such love' before in his life. Daveggio closed his statement by acknowledging that he thought about his actions every day and does feel remorse over them. Michaud on the other hand, adhering to her attorneys' advice, did not respond to any statement or make a comment.

Vanessa Samson's mother, Christina Samson, spoke about the irreparable damage her daughter's death had caused in their lives. She stated that her daughter had a lot to live for. Her friends spoke about how she brought joy into a lot of people's lives and nothing would ever be the same again.

Before the sentence was given out, Nicole Samson, the victim's sister, was questioned outside the court about the possible punishment for the killers; she stated that it was 'in the hands of the jury, the judge and God.'

Sentencing

In September 2002, Michelle Lyn Michaud and James Anthony Daveggio were sentenced to death by a jury consisting of four men and eight women at the Alameda County Superior Court. The jury decided upon a death sentence for the couple in the light of all the evidence of torture and rape in twenty-two-year-old Vanessa Lei Samson's murder.

Throughout the proceedings, both the law enforcement agencies and the state prosecutors emphasized that it would be the right outcome considering all the atrocities. The verdict came after a long wait for the family of the victim. Despite the fact that capital punishment is frowned upon across the country, this was one case where perhaps nobody protested against it. Everyone was sympathetic to the plight of the dead girl as well as the other victims.

The question in the minds of the people was, how could anybody possibly do this to an innocent girl? During the sentencing hearing, the state prosecutors revealed that Vanessa Samson had almost averted the couple, but Daveggio made his partner turn around so he could pick up the beautiful young girl walking by herself.

On the day the penalty was given, Alameda County Superior Court Judge Larry Goodman presided over the proceedings of the court and announced the final verdict. The jury responsible for the conviction raised the possibility of capital punishment in June. After the decision had been read, Judge Goodman went on record to say that he agreed with the jury and it was the right thing. They had been responsible for a heinous crime that was unfathomable in all ways.

The couple was sadistic and absolutely merciless, which ultimately led to the argument that no mercy should be shown toward them. Both Daveggio and Michaud had ensured that there was no way Samson could have been rescued or found alive. During the assault and torture, she had been forced to wear a rubber ball gag so she could not call out for help or make any noise.

The gruesome details which came forward led the jury to recommend the death sentence for the couple. Initially, James Daveggio and Michelle Michaud had been arrested on account of rape as they had been found responsible for assaulting a young girl in Reno. As more victims came forward, the Reno case proceeded to the U.S District Court where Michaud was eventually sentenced to confinement. Daveggio was brought up on the same charges with double counts of rape as well as assault.

During the Vanessa Samson murder and rape trial, the Reno victim, along with the couple's previous targets, agreed to testify in front of the jury. They were going to recount the details of what had happened with them so that the court could come to an adequate decision in the case of Samson's murder.

Throughout the proceedings, Vincent Samson had strong faith in America's justice system. He knew that his sister's death was not going to go unpunished and even stated in open court that Daveggio 'deserved to die.' On the day of the sentencing, the courtroom was filled with Vanessa Samson's friends and family members. Deputy District Attorney Angela Backers had led the prosecution side and presented key evidence that ultimately resulted in the jury deliberating over a death penalty for two days and finally handing it out.

Backers told the jury that the two found gratification in their crimes. The rapes and murder was regarded as a cat-and-mouse game where the two sought the thrill of torturing their victims until they grew bored. As it was in Vanessa Samson's case, the couple was looking to switch things up a bit and escalate from rape to murder. Law enforcement agencies had recovered the saliva-stained gag as well as the bloodied curling irons from the minivan where Samson was restrained. Angela Backers established that both of these tools were used as torture instruments to subdue and rape the victim.

James Anthony Daveggio and Michelle Lyn Michaud were convicted of first degree murder under special circumstances, murder in the commission of rape, on May 6, 2002. Soon afterwards, the jury decided to recommend a death penalty for the gruesome murder and rape by instrument. The decision was spurred by further revelations that Vanessa Samson had been the sixth victim in a series of brutal assaults that had lasted a span of three months and crossed state lines. The unfortunate girl was their only murder victim, but five others had barely managed to escape.

After the sentencing, Michelle Michaud became the fourteenth woman to await her execution on death row in California. She was taken to the women's quarters within the female prison at Chowchilla. It is expected that Michaud will spend the remaining time confined in this jail.

A Psychological Profile

The serial raping and killing of James Anthony Daveggio and Michelle Lyn Michaud drew interest from psychological experts and profilers across the country. This was a case that stood out amongst America's crime history. The acts of torture they had subjected their victims to were gruesome and incredibly brutal. While the victimization was similar to Gerald Gallego and other serial killers in the past, Michaud's role in the crime was what captured the attention of the law enforcement agencies as well as psychological analysts.

Before Vanessa Samson's case, there were no reported cases of rapes or assault where the perpetrator had been a woman engaging in the act. While there had been male-female serial killer couples in the past, the woman was mostly submissive in the relationship, with her part restricted to luring in the victims.

However, Michelle Michaud changed the way serial crime teams would be regarded in the future. She not only initiated the sexual torture and assaults, but she also dominated her partner. It was deduced from victim testimonies that Daveggio usually left the decision making to Michaud. He also let her take charge of the situation, be it driving from one town to another or choosing a target.

Juanita Rodriguez recounted to the authorities that when she was begging to be let go alive, she appealed to the woman, making up a false story of being mother to a nine-month-old baby. According to Rodriguez, the woman seemed sympathetic after asking a few questions and realizing that there was a child who needed to be looked after. When Daveggio asked her what they should do with the victim, Michaud appeared to deliberate for a minute and then finally decided to let Juanita Rodriguez go.

As was evident from the girl's traumatic account, between Daveggio and Michaud, the latter was in charge of making important decisions, such as what to do with the victims in the end. Like Rodriguez, there were other victims who also had similar stories to share. The common factor in all of those was Michaud's increasingly aggressive streak.

In seventeen-year-old Patty Wilson's case, Michelle Michaud was the assailant as well as the ever-present looming threat that forced the young girl to stick to the fake story she reported to her manager and the police. When Wilson agreed to lie about what she had endured that night, Michaud ripped the girl's shirt to make it appear real. The woman had taken to criminal life like a fish to water. She knew how to terrify the victims and make sure that they remained silent. While Daveggio incurred the violence physically, Michaud traumatized them emotionally.

Her threatening, raspy voice remained with each of the victims long after they had been dropped off. Psychological experts concluded that Michaud was indeed very much in control of the situation and did not consent to just being in the background. She wanted to be as much a part of everything as Daveggio; in fact, her urges were even more powerful than his. Wilson stated that it was Michaud who had come up with the false story and had torn her shirt for effect, making it clear that the woman assailant did not shy away from any challenge. This made her all the more dangerous and fearsome.

The conflict in her personality was such that it boggled the minds of analysts and profilers. They failed to pinpoint the exact cause of the turmoil or isolate any one factor which caused her to take such a turn. The question remained, did she suffer from a multiple personality disorder or was she a ruthless sociopath all along, hiding beneath a polished façade?

Who was Michelle Michaud really?

Nobody could actually come up with an answer to that question, other than what had already been determined. In the eyes of the world, she had begun as a well-paid prostitute whose actions were initially the result of methamphetamines and other hard drugs. As a young, rebellious girl, she went through several failed relationships with abusive partners, finally finding her place with Daveggio. The tattooed gang member gave her the home life she may have always aspired to possess. She may have realized that she would not do better than him and, hence, made it her life's aim to keep him happy and satisfied at all times.

At the very beginning, Michaud was the submissive partner that Daveggio always wanted. However, once she ventured into the world of crime, she became aware of her potential. The woman would no longer settle for keeping her partner happy. Their spree was as much about her fulfillment as it was his.

Her role as a mother was also keenly observed by the experts and analysts. While she may not have been a model mother, the accounts of her earlier life implied that she did take care of her young daughters and looked after them. All that changed drastically when Daveggio entered her life. It was as if her motherly instincts were completely eclipsed by her desire for that man. She let his drug dealer friend set up shop in their house despite the presence of her children.

One of the duo's earliest victims was a 13-year-old friend of Michaud's daughter. Nancy Baker later stated that Michaud forced her into the room where Daveggio was waiting to rape her. She later joined in as well. While her partner might have been detached from the victim, Michaud herself knew the girl quite well. Baker visited their house frequently and was on close terms with the family.

Her progression has been charted by analysts who claim that the victimization of Nancy Baker was symbolic to her fading rationality. She lost all ability to connect or empathize with anyone. It got to the point where her own daughter's suffering pleased her.

Yet somehow, Juanita Rodriguez's appeal managed to sway her. Once she found that their victim might be a mother, Michaud decided to let her go. It could be the last remaining shred of humaneness that prompted the decision or just an error in judgment since Rodriguez was the victim who played a huge role in the couple's arrest on account of rape and assault in Reno, Nevada. Experts and profilers also believed that Juanita Rodriguez's release was only made possible because they did not have any plans to kill their victims as yet.

Michelle Michaud's personality was one of the most perplexing contradictions that the psychological and criminal experts had come across.

It was unanimously agreed upon that there was no emotion or remorse involved in the decision to let any of their victims go, especially as far as Michaud was concerned. While Daveggio may have expressed his remorse during one or two of the early encounters, his partner was completely devoid of any display of guilt or weakness. In the beginning of their spree, one of their victims stated that Daveggio even seemed to apologize for hurting her and causing the trauma but quickly overcame his emotional admission as Michaud diverted his attention to the problem of dealing with their victim.

As the crime spree spiraled out of control, it claimed several victims, who all appeared as easy targets. Daveggio and Michaud usually chose girls who were on their own and abducted them from sparsely populated locations. Vanessa Samson was the only victim taken from an area where possible witnesses could have been present. It seemed as if, by the end, Michaud was beginning to enjoy the acts of torture and abuse more than her partner. When her daughter was calling out to her for help, she warned her to 'keep quiet' and ordered the girl to submit. Experts and analysts were of the opinion that she became sexually aroused during the incident.

As the details of all the rapes and assaults unraveled, it was almost no surprise that the couple had killed Vanessa Samson in such a brutal and vicious manner at the end. The twenty-two-year-old girl's murder may have been the culmination of all the angst and turmoil that had caused them to go on a spree of serial rapes and assaults lasting almost three months.

Deputy District Attorney Angela Backers stated in court that the couple intended to create a name for themselves. It was only a matter of time until they murdered someone; and unfortunately, Vanessa Samson was the one they went for. According to Backers, the evidence recovered signified that Daveggio and Michaud had already decided that their next victim was not going to be let off since the authorities were closing in and their desire to kill was at its peak.

The serial raping and killing of James

Anthony Daveggio and Michelle Lyn Michaud surpassed everything that the law enforcement agencies and crime experts believed to be true. Their history and troubled background is testimony to the fact that they both should have been behind bars much earlier in life or at least within the walls of a psychiatric facility. While Michaud did not draw any attention to herself during her adulthood, Daveggio managed to raise red flags on numerous occasions. It was by coincidence and strategy that he escaped the sex offender alert. His partner, on the other hand, did not show up as a suspect in criminal activity until much later.

Unabashedly, they continued to play out their relationship fantasies, eventually going from living in a house to moving around constantly in their minivan. Michaud remained a mystery which slowly began to unravel in the end as everything began to fall apart for the couple.

Experts and analysts debated over what bonded the two together so strongly. In the beginning of their relationship, it seemed as if the two was another one of those 'opposites attract' pairings. One was a rugged gang member who rode around on a stolen Harley-Davidson, the other, a sophisticated prostitute with a certain command over the spoken language. Experts noted that what was interesting about Michaud was the fact that she did not flaunt her line of work by her appearance or social behavior. For an onlooker, she might have been a conservative, middle-class woman reaching for the American dream.

Unlike her boyfriend, Michaud could engage people without raising any alarms. While Daveggio made constant grammatical errors and slurred his sentences, Michaud's conversational skills were top notch, and rarely did she make mistakes with her grammar. Later on, it was suggested that the two became close due to the sexual nature of their relationship. According to FBI profilers, sexual desire and gratification can be a pivotal factor in any relationship, particularly if it's between two budding criminals.

Psychological experts have found another fascinating development in the early lives of both Daveggio and Michaud. During their respective teen years, it was quite a role reversal. As per his fellow high school classmates, James Anthony Daveggio came across as a polite boy with deep blue eyes, which made it easier for the girls to trust him. Michaud, on the other hand, was a striking contradiction. She was abrasive, rebellious and did not have many friends either in school or around the neighborhood. It was the boy who was covering his underlying sociopathic tendencies at the time, while the girl displayed no inhibitions whatsoever. Young Michaud's indiscretions were already known and heard of by every acquaintance and family member.

Later on, both Daveggio and Michaud took on different personalities, hence prompting the debate that they were harboring a multiple personality disorder. It was Daveggio whose violence and aggression resulted in frequent brawls with his fellow schoolboys, causing public concern. Michaud somehow managed to rein in her rebellion and take on the portrayal of a relatively friendly woman. She built a relationship with her mother, even going on shopping trips and to restaurants, just like any other mother-daughter relationship.

The murderous killer that had been lurking inside Daveggio was threatening to come out. Even though Daveggio had kept a lid on that side of his personality, it was always clawing at him. During the investigation into his background, the authorities implied that, as a youngster, he might have been responsible for the assault on Cassie Riley that claimed her young life.

Furthermore, it was discovered that Daveggio could be linked to a few other unsolved murders and rapes. His police records showed that he had pleaded guilty to a couple of offenses as well. It was surprising that, despite his deteriorating mental stability, the psychiatric evaluation had concluded that nothing was wrong with him. There were a few experts and analysts who said that Daveggio's reports were clear because he was not psychologically ill at the time. He had been intent on acting out the sexual fantasies his mind conjured as the urges became overwhelming, fueled by Ihde's presence in his life.

Serial rapist and murderer Michael Ihde was

caught and convicted after claiming the lives of innocent victims, much like his friend, James Anthony Daveggio. When Michaud came into his life, she was far from a calming influence. After the two began dating, his violent demeanor and aggression proceeded to worsen instead of subsiding.

There was no way to go but downwards for the both of them. Daveggio began to project his desires and twisted fantasies upon Michaud. Soon enough, she gave in and followed him. While Michaud might have been initially working out of the desire to salvage their relationship, Daveggio aimed for a serial killer partnership similar to Gerald and Charlene Gallego. However, neither one managed to achieve anything that they had in mind. Michelle Michaud spiraled down a path of darkness and cruelty while Daveggio became the other half of a deadly team who terrorized innocent young girls across California and Nevada.

Crime experts began to search for a possible trigger that might have led to their sudden recklessness with Samson. Before murdering her, they had let all their victims go. While the police closing in was a huge factor behind the couple's acceleration, analysts believe there was a psychological aspect to it as well. They had been raping and assaulting their victims for almost two months, toying with the idea of murder. Once they came to Pleasanton, California, Daveggio believed that it would be the ideal place for their first kill. He had grown up and spent most of his life in this town, and it was like coming full circle for him.

For Michaud, the situation had transgressed. By now, she was deriving pleasure in the acts of violence, and murder seemed the likely next step in her thrill-seeking spree. Michaud had become brazen and overconfident that they would never be caught. As the two maneuvered around the authorities, it did appear as if the two would manage to continue their terrorizing journey onward.

Thankfully, that did not happen and the police apprehended them. Neither Michaud nor Daveggio could have imagined that their first murder victim would also be their last. After Vanessa Samson, they had no intention of stopping. Yet, despite their best efforts to evade jail and long term arrest, it was all over.

Surprisingly, it was Michaud who gave away critical information linking both her and Daveggio to Samson's kidnapping and subsequent death. Law enforcement officials already feared that Daveggio and Michaud were behind this heinous crime, but they did not have any certainty of proof. It wasn't until Michaud broke down in prison upon watching the news report and confessed to her cellmate that she was in 'trouble,' that the detectives and FBI agents discovered the truth. The fact that it was Michaud who succumbed first under pressure was quite an unusual development in the case. Up till now, she had been the one in control and in charge of the situation.

It was not like her to relent or display weakness, particularly when things were looking so dire.

Perhaps the reason that she broke was that she realized it was the end. They were not going to get away with their crimes anymore. She had been isolated from her partner and it was all over for the two of them. This could have triggered her turmoil and caused her enough distress to divulge information regarding Samson. Experts could argue that Michaud's confession may have even been spurred by guilt. She was caught and in prison; all the doors were closing in on her, and she knew that it was not going to end well for her. Hence, when she heard that Vanessa Samson had been found dead, the guilt of her actions overwhelmed her.

However, that is one far-fetched theory. The popular opinion about Michelle Michaud is that there wasn't a guilty or remorseful bone in her body. She did not feel regret for anything she had done. When the police caught and arrested Daveggio and Michaud for rape and assault, the only thing that concerned her was finding a way out. She did not intend to stay in prison for long and wanted to be out as soon as possible. Her previous encounters with the police had led her to believe that there was a possibility of serving a short-term sentence and securing release.

Experts and profilers believe that when she saw the news report and deduced that the police were conducting an investigation into Samson's murder, she knew that it could implicate her. According to her cellmate, Michaud started to cry and then admitted that something was gravely wrong. All of a sudden, the woman who had expressed no emotion as yet was breaking down. However, it was all momentary. The police and investigators claimed that she seemed to give up information readily during the interviews. Experts tried to explain her behavior from various aspects.

Many thought that she wanted redemption, while others believed that it was another ploy. Michaud was either trying to throw clues to the police that would only lead them to Daveggio, or she wanted a deal in exchange for helping the police with the murder investigation. Perhaps she had convinced herself that there was still a way for her to get ahead. It appeared that Michaud had become so distant from reality that she could not gauge what was happening around her. After a day of interviewing, the police officers and detectives had already reached the conclusion that Michaud and her partner, Daveggio, were Samson's murderers.

However, Michaud still seemed oblivious to the fact that her story was over. There was not going to be the ending that she wanted or hoped for. Michaud had admitted to the truth and she would never be able to retreat from it.

If she did admit to the information herself, it would not be that much of a shock. The woman's mind was a mystery to everyone. She was a bold and dominant woman who believed that she did not have to adhere to any rules. Psychological experts believe that she was so wrapped up in her own sense of superiority that by divulging the information to the investigating officials, she may have been trying to gain some lost ground.

There are others who opine that Michaud took pride in her actions, which is perhaps why she admitted her involvement in Samson's murder. On a previous occasion, when she saw Juanita Rodriguez's incident being reported on TV, she proudly boasted about it in front of her daughter and Nancy Baker. In her statement, the young girl went on record to say that when she was at Daveggio and Michaud's house and the details regarding Juanita Rodriguez's abduction and rape were reported, she heard Michaud announce, "We did that."

While initially Michaud may have been inclined to reveal the information regarding Samson, she changed her stance completely as the investigation was handed over to federal authorities. She did not shy away from trying everything she could to get away.

There was no doubt that the woman was devious, sociopathic and devoid of any moral fiber which could cause her to exercise some humanity. During the trial, her statements were also used to charge and convict Daveggio. The two were separated at last, but not without wreaking havoc and causing long-lasting trauma to their victims. A young innocent life that was full of hopes and dreams for the future was lost.

While the death penalty may have come as justice being served at the end, it would do little to fill the void that Vanessa Samson's death left in the lives of her loved ones. She caught the eye of the deadly demons on her way to work, but unlike their previous victims, she did not get to escape.

Both Daveggio and Michaud were overtaken by a strong desire to kill and they knew that the timing was perfect with the holidays settling in. Samson was their last victim and one who will be remembered as one of the most brutal murders in America's serial crime history.

Other Books By RJ Parker

Experience a thought-provoking and engrossing read with books from RJ Parker Publishing. Featuring the work of crime writer and publisher RJ Parker, as well as many other authors, our company features exciting True CRIME and CRIME Fiction books in eBook, Paperback, and Audiobook editions.

rjpp.ca/RJ-PARKER-BOOKS

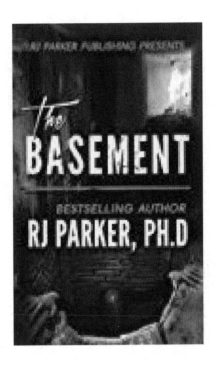

On March 24, 1987, the Philadelphia Police Department received a phone call from a woman who stated that she had been held captive for the last four months. When police officers arrived at the pay phone from which the call was made, Josefina Rivera told them that she and three other women had been held captive in a basement by a man named Gary Heidnik. This is a shocking story of kidnapping, rape, torture, mutilation, dismemberment, decapitation, and murder.

The subject matter in this book is graphic

Amazon Links- *eBook* | *Paperback* | *Audiobook*

The ultimate reference for anyone compelled by the pathology and twisted minds behind the most disturbing of homicidal monsters. From A to Z, and from around the world, these serial killers have killed in excess of 3,000 innocent victims, affecting thousands of friends and family members. There are monsters in this book that you may not have heard of, but you won't forget them after reading their stories. This reference book will make a great collection for true crime aficionados.

WARNING: *There are 15 dramatic crime scene photos in this book that some may find extremely disturbing*

Amazon Links- *eBook | Paperback | Audiobook*

This collection of 'filicidal killers' provides a gripping overview of how things can go horribly wrong in once-loving families. Parents Who Killed their Children depicts ten of the most notorious and horrific cases of homicidal parental units out of control, people like Andrea Yates, Diane Downs, Susan Smith, and Jeffrey MacDonald who received a great deal of media attention. The author explores the reasons, from addiction to postpartum psychosis, insanity to altruism, revenge and jealousy. Each story is detailed with background information on the parents, the murder scenes, trials, sentencing and aftermath.

SUSPENSE MAGAZINE - "*Parents Who Kill Their Children is a great read for aficionados of true crime. The way the author laid the cases out made the hair on the back of my neck stand up.*"

Amazon Links- *eBook | Paperback | Audiobook*

Acknowledgements

Thank you to my editor, proofreaders, and cover artist for your support:

~ RJ

Aeternum Designs (book cover)

Bettye McKee (editor)

Lee Knieper Husemann

Robyn MacEachern

Valerie Hartling

Laura Martin

Gail Chen

Andrea Strickland Carver

Linda H. Bergeron

Marlene Fabregas

Kathi Garcia

Sandra Miller

About the Author

RJ Parker, Ph.D., is an award-winning and bestselling true crime author and owner of RJ Parker Publishing, Inc. He has written over 25 true crime books which are available in eBook, paperback and audiobook editions, and have sold in over 100 countries. He holds certifications in Serial Crime, Criminal Profiling and a Ph.D. in Criminology.

To date, RJ has donated over 3,000 autographed books to allied troops serving overseas and to our wounded warriors recovering in Naval and Army hospitals all over the world. He also donates to

Victims of Violent Crimes Canada.

If you are a police officer, firefighter, paramedic or serve in the military, active or retired, RJ gives his eBooks freely in appreciation for your service.

Contact Information

Author's Email:

AuthorRJParker@gmail.com

Publisher's Email:

Agent@RJParkerPublishing.com

Website:

http://m.RJPARKERPUBLISHING.com/

Twitter:

http://www.Twitter.com/realRJParker

Facebook:

https://www.Facebook.com/AuthorRJParker

Amazon Author's Page:

rjpp.ca/RJ-PARKER-BOOKS

References

1. Female Serial Killers: How and Why Women Become Monsters by Peter Vronsky, **ISBN-13:** 978-0425213902
2. Ranker.com – Serial Couples
3. Psychology Today: Serial Killer Couples - The Human Equation
4. http://murderpedia.org/female.M/m/michaud-michelle.htm
5. http://www.crimezzz.net/serialkillers/D/DEV EGGIO_james_MICHAUD_michelle.php